Spring Harvest
Bible Workbook

RUTH

Love, Honour and Obey

Elizabeth McQuoid

Series editor for Bible character workbooks – Ian Coffey

LIFESTYLE

Equipping the Church for action

First published in 2003 Spring Harvest Publishing Division and Authentic Lifestyle

09 08 07 06 05 04 03   7 6 5 4 3 2 1

Authentic Lifestyle is an imprint of Authentic Media

PO Box 300, Carlisle, Cumbria, CA3 0QS, UK

and Box 1047, Waynesboro, GA 30830-2047, USA

www.paternoster-publishing.com

British Library Cataloguing in Publication Data

A catalogue record for this book is available from the British Library

ISBN 1-85078-536-8

Typeset by Spring Harvest
Cover design by Diane Bainbridge
Printed in Great Britain by Bell and Bain Ltd., Glasgow

CONTENTS

About this book   4

Introduction to Ruth   7

Session One: Tragedy strikes   8

Session Two: Acts of kindness   12

Session Three: Family loyalty   16

Session Four: Difficult decisions   20

Session Five: Family heritage   24

Session Six: A happy ending   28

Leader's Guide

Introduction   32

Session One: notes   36

Session Two: notes   38

Session Three: notes   40

Session Four: notes   42

Session Five: notes   44

Session Six: notes   46

Further Information   48

ABOUT THIS BOOK

This book is written primarily for a group situation, but can easily be used by individuals who want to study the book of Ruth. It can be used in a variety of contexts, so it is perhaps helpful to spell out the assumptions that we have made about the groups that will use it. These can have a variety of names – homegroups, Bible study groups, cell groups – we've used housegroup as the generic term.

▶ The emphasis of the studies will be on the application of the Bible. Group members will not just learn facts, but will be encouraged to think 'How does this apply to me? What change does it require of me? What incidents or situations in my life is this relevant to?'

▶ Housegroups can encourage honesty and make space for questions and doubts. The aim of the studies is not to find the 'right answer', but to help members understand the Bible by working through their questions. The Christian faith throws up paradoxes. Events in people's lives may make particular verses difficult to understand. The housegroup should be a safe place to express these concerns.

▶ Housegroups can give opportunities for deep friendships to develop. Group members will be encouraged to talk about their experiences, feelings, questions, hopes and fears. They will be able to offer one another pastoral support and to get involved in each other's lives.

▶ There is a difference between being a collection of individuals who happen to meet together every Wednesday and being an effective group who bounce ideas off each other, spark inspiration and creativity, pooling their talents and resources to create solutions together: one whose whole is definitely greater than the sum of its parts. The process of working through these studies will encourage healthy group dynamics.

Space is given for you to write answers, comments, questions and thoughts. This book will not tell you what to think, but will help you discover the truth of God's word through thinking, discussing, praying and listening.

FOR GROUP MEMBERS

▶ You will probably get more out of the study if you spend some time during the week reading the passage and thinking about the questions. Make a note of anything you don't understand.

▶ Pray that God will help you to understand the passage and show you how to apply it. Pray for other members in the group too, that they will find the study helpful.

▶ Be willing to take part in the discussions. The leader of the group is not there as an expert with all the answers. They will want everyone to get involved and share their thoughts and opinions.

▶ However, don't dominate the group! If you are aware that you are saying a lot, make space for others to contribute. Be sensitive to other group members and aim to be encouraging. If you disagree with someone, say so but without putting down their contribution.

FOR INDIVIDUALS

▶ Although this book is written with a group in mind, it can also easily be used by individuals. You obviously won't be able to do the group activities suggested, but you can consider how you would answer the questions and write your thoughts in the space provided.

▶ You may find it helpful to talk to a prayer partner about what you have learnt, and ask them to pray for you as you try and apply what you are learning to your life.

▶ The New International Version of the text is printed in the book. If you use a different version, then read from your own Bible as well.

Other titles in this Spring Harvest Bible Studies series:

Sermon on the Mount – ISBN 1-85078-407-8
Based on the Spring Harvest 2000 theme, A Royal Banquet.

Jesus at the Centre – ISBN 1-85078-440-X
Based on the Spring Harvest 2001 theme, King of the Hill.

Letters to the Churches – ISBN 1-85078-441-8
Based on the Spring Harvest 2002 theme, You've Got Mail.

Big Themes from Colossians – ISBN 1-85078-457-4
Based on the Spring Harvest 1999 theme, Across the Borderline.

Mission of God – ISBN 1-85078-496-5
Based on the Spring Harvest 2003 theme, Shepherd's Bush to King's Cross.

David – After God's Own Heart – ISBN 1-85078-497-3
Based on selected chapters from Ian Coffey's book,
The Story of David, ISBN 1-85078-485-X.

Jonah – God's Compassion – ISBN 1-85078-508-2
Studies on Jonah.

Moses – Friend of God – ISBN 1-85078-519-8
Studies on Moses.

Connect! Workbook – ISBN 1-85078-521-X
Based on Tim Jeffery and Steve Chalke's ground-breaking book rethinking mission for the 21st century.

INTRODUCTION TO RUTH

Life in the Promised Land had not turned out to be the 'milk and honey' experience the Israelites had in mind.

But they only had themselves to blame.

Instead of ridding the land of the Canaanites as God had commanded, they had allowed them to stay in the land. Compromise soon followed. The moral and spiritual decay that had set in was now spiralling out of control. Years of disobedience towards God were reaping their harvest and a disturbingly familiar pattern was beginning to emerge. Every time the Israelites threatened to be overwhelmed by their enemies, they cried out to God for help and each time he graciously sent a judge to deliver them. But once the emergency had been averted, the people soon descended into apostasy again.

Whilst the people seemed to lurch from one crisis to another, God had a long-term rescue plan in mind. His plan turned out to be a rags-to-riches love story. The story began with a family crisis – a widow mourning the loss and livelihood of her husband and two sons. The only silver lining in this cloud of grief was her devoted daughter-in-law, Ruth. Quite out of the blue, life changed for these two desolate women when Ruth found love in the harvest fields.

Ruth's marriage and new family delighted all the neighbours and friends in Bethlehem but it was actually only a single scene in a much larger love story – the story of God's love for the world. As it turned out, Ruth was the great-grandmother of King David, Jesus' ancestor. And Jesus demonstrated the greatest act of love ever known. His death on the cross in our place was God's once-and-for-all rescue plan for humanity.

It seems that God delights in taking unlikely characters like Ruth and inviting us to be part of his plan. As Ruth proved, involvement isn't dependent on family background, race or religious credentials: it is simply about putting our faith in God and being obedient to him. Today God invites us to trust him and become part of the greatest love story ever told!

TRAGEDY STRIKES

AIM

Aim: To learn how to find hope in God in times of crisis

'Crisis' is one of the most popular words of our generation. We talk of a political crisis, an economic crisis, a work crisis and even a family crisis. And at some point in life, a crisis will touch each of us. In those times, how do we find the strength to keep on going? The answer is hope. The story of Ruth reminds us that even in the deepest crisis God offers us hope. He alone can bring something good out of a tragedy.

> *In the days when the judges ruled, there was a famine in the land, and a man from Bethlehem in Judah, together with his wife and two sons, went to live for a while in the country of Moab. The man's name was Elimelech, and his wife's name Naomi, and the names of his two sons were Mahlon and Kilion. They were Ephrathites from Bethlehem, Judah. And they went to Moab and lived there.*
>
> *Now Elimelech, Naomi's husband, died, and she was left with her two sons. They married Moabite women, one named Orpah and the other Ruth. After they had lived there about ten years, both Mahlon and Kilion also died, and Naomi was left without her two sons and her husband.*
>
> **Ruth 1:1–5**

TO SET THE SCENE
We all face difficulties in life and cope with them in different ways. Think back to a particular 'crisis' in your life. What helped you keep going?

- Someone praying for you
- Someone bringing a meal round
- Listening to a sermon
- Something else

Explain how these words or actions helped you find hope in the middle of your crisis.

READ RUTH 1:1-22

1 Describe the moral and spiritual crisis that was facing the nation of Israel in the time of the Judges.

2 Look at the crisis that has hit Naomi's family in 1:1-5. In 1:21, Naomi describes herself as 'empty' – is this a good description?

3 Naomi attributes her sorrows to God in 1:20-21. Is this valid?

4 To what extent is God responsible for the difficulties in our lives?

5 Naomi felt that Ruth's returning with her to Bethlehem would just add to the family crisis. What was her reasoning?

6 In times of crisis it is often difficult to know how to respond. In those times, our true character and faith in God are shown for what they are. What aspect of your spiritual life or your character would you like to work on so that you are more prepared to handle crises?

7 Despite this tragic family crisis, what are the signs of hope in this chapter?

8 Look at the following verses. What hope do they give you for your own situation?

- ▶ Lamentations 3:19-26
- ▶ Romans 8:28
- ▶ Romans 15:13
- ▶ 2 Corinthians 4:7-8
- ▶ 2 Corinthians 12:7-10

APPLY THIS TO
MY CHURCH

9 What practical steps can the church take to help families facing crisis?

APPLY THIS TO
MY CHURCH

10 Spend some time in prayer for families and individuals in your church or group who are facing difficult situations.

WORSHIP

Give each person time to reflect on their personal situation. Naomi spoke of the Almighty (*El-Shaddai*, the powerful one) and the Lord (*Yahweh*, 'I am who I am', the ever-present and unchanging God). Pray these names of God into your own situation. Then read through Psalm 13 together and thank God for his constant love, salvation and goodness that are realities regardless of our circumstances. If it is appropriate, in twos, petition God to intervene in your current difficulties.

FURTHER STUDY

There are many books written on the subject of pain and suffering. Two well-known books are *The Problem of Pain* by C.S. Lewis and *Disappointment with God* by Philip Yancey.

FOR NEXT WEEK

Look back to your answer to question 6. This week put practical measures in place to help you work on a particular aspect of your spiritual life or character. See if you're able to handle the stressful points in your week differently as a result!

ACTS OF KINDNESS

Aim: To recognise God's kindness to us and share it with others

The saying goes 'there's no such thing as a free lunch'. And it's true – when people give us something they generally expect something back in return. When was the last time someone showed you kindness ... just because? In fact, we're often so busy that our eyes are closed to other people's needs and struggles. The book of Ruth challenges us to get our priorities right in this area. It reminds us that showing kindness is costly but important, as it mirrors God's character to our world. How else will the world know what God is like unless we show them?

Boaz replied, 'I've been told all about what you have done for your mother-in-law since the death of your husband – how you left your father and mother and your homeland and came to live with a people you did not know before. May the Lord repay you for what you have done. May you be richly rewarded by the Lord, the God of Israel, under whose wings you have come to take refuge.'

'May I continue to find favour in your eyes, my lord,' she said. 'You have given me comfort and have spoken kindly to your servant – though I do not have the standing of one of your servant girls.'

Ruth 2:11–13

TO SET THE SCENE
Brainstorm together and come up with a definition of 'kindness' that you all agree on. Who is usually first to show you kindness? Your:

▶ Family
▶ Neighbours
▶ Colleagues at work
▶ Church members
▶ Non-Christian friends

READ RUTH 2:1-23

1 'Kindness' is a key theme throughout the book. At this point in the story, how have Ruth and Boaz demonstrated kindness to others?

The Hebrew word *hesed,* found in Ruth 1:8, 2:20, and 3:10 means steadfast love, kindness, and mercy. It was used to describe relationships between individuals but also of God's relationship with his covenant people.

2 What were the risks involved in Ruth showing kindness to Naomi?

3 In 2:20, Naomi recognises God's kindness to her and Ruth. Looking back over the chapter, how has God shown his kindness to the pair? Look at his activity in:
- ❱ The decisions taken by the characters
- ❱ The apparent coincidences in the story

WHAT DOES SEARCH THE BIBLE SAY?

4 God's kindness to Ruth is particularly significant because she was a foreigner from the land of Moab. What can you find out about the history of this nation and what God felt about them? Look at Genesis 19: 30-38, Deuteronomy 23:3.

5 How had Ruth become part of the family of God? Look at 1:16-17.

WHAT DOES SEARCH THE BIBLE SAY?

6 What comes to your mind when you imagine God's 'wings of refuge' 2:12? Look also at Psalm 17:8, 91:4, Luke 13:34.

7 What lessons do we learn about evangelism from the fact that God extends his wings of refuge to foreigners like Ruth?

ENGAGING WITH THE WORLD **8** What role does showing kindness play in evangelism? Look at John 13:35.

HOW DOES THIS APPLY TO ME **9** Like Naomi, it is often only in retrospect that we can recognise God's kindness in our life. Take an A4 sheet of paper and as you reflect on your life, jot down all the examples you can remember of God's special kindness to you. Share some of your recollections with the group.

WORSHIP

Meditate together on the image of the Lord's 'wings of refuge'. Sing, or listen to, songs on this theme if helpful. Share together what picture of God this image gives you and thank him for being this kind of God to you. (Look at Exodus 19:4 for a further reference to God's wings.) Then pray for those who take refuge under your wings – it could be your children, the children in your Sunday school class, the others who serve in the ministry you lead, the older folk you look after. Pray that your care and protection of them would be a reflection of how God looks after you.

FURTHER STUDY

People give and receive loving kindness in different ways. To learn more about this read Gary Chapman's *The Five Love Languages*.

FOR NEXT WEEK

Have everyone in the group write their names on a piece of paper and fold them up. Put the slips of paper in a bowl and then take turns taking a name from the bowl. Don't tell anyone whose name you have and if you pick your own name put it back in the bowl and choose again. This week do an act of kindness to the person whose name you have picked. You could deliver a meal to their home, offer to pick their children up from school, invite them for a game of squash – any small act of kindness to demonstrate that you care for them.

ACTIVITY PAGE

'Loving kindness' looks different in different situations. Consider the following scenarios. How could you show 'loving kindness' in these situations and what factors would hold you back?

- ▶ You have a young family. Your spouse's widowed mother is becoming less and less able to take care of herself. The wider family are getting together to discuss how to take care of her. What would you suggest and what are the options?

- ▶ New neighbours have just moved in next door. How could you make them feel welcome in the area?

- ▶ There is a couple in their late thirties who have been to your church for about two years. On Sunday, you learn that the man's father has died suddenly. The father was not a Christian. You know the couple, have had a meal in their home, but don't feel you know them that well. What would you do in this situation?

FAMILY LOYALTY

AIM

Aim: To investigate the role of kinsman-redeemer and reflect how Christ has been that to us

How would you rate your relationship with your extended family? Do you just meet up at weddings and funerals or does your wider family provide a network of support and encouragement? In Old Testament times the kinsman-redeemer played a vital role in protecting and promoting family life. Whether we have a family who supports us like this or not, when we're part of God's family Jesus is always acting on our behalf – he truly is our kinsman-redeemer!

> *When Boaz had finished eating and drinking and was in good spirits, he went over to lie down at the far end of the grain pile. Ruth approached quietly, uncovered his feet and lay down. In the middle of the night something startled the man, and he turned and discovered a woman lying at his feet.*
>
> *'Who are you?' he asked.*
>
> *'I am your servant Ruth,' she said. 'Spread the corner of your garment over me, since you are a kinsman-redeemer.'*
>
> *'The Lord bless you, my daughter,' he replied. 'This kindness is greater than that which you showed earlier: you have not run after the younger men, whether rich or poor. And now, my daughter, don't be afraid. I will do for you all that you ask. All my fellow townsmen know that you are a woman of noble character. Although it is true that I am near of kin, there is a kinsman-redeemer nearer than I. Stay here for the night, and in the morning if he wants to redeem, good; let him redeem. But if he is not willing, as surely as the Lord lives I will do it. Lie here until morning.'*
>
> **Ruth 3:7–13**

TO SET THE SCENE

The kinsman-redeemer was essentially the relative who was responsible for rescuing the family out of a difficult situation. Share together examples of when you have been rescued. These could be serious or funny memories, times when you were rescued by a family member or someone else.

READ RUTH 3:1-18

ENGAGING WITH ... THE WORLD

1 'Redeemer' is a key concept in the Book of Ruth. Brainstorm how you would explain it to a non-Christian.

WHAT DOES ... SEARCH THE BIBLE SAY?

2 The kinsman-redeemer was responsible for looking after the needy members of the extended family. Look at the following references to find out what his role included:

- ▶ Leviticus 25:25
- ▶ Leviticus 25:47-49
- ▶ Numbers 35:19-21
- ▶ Deuteronomy 25:5-6

3 In this situation, what did Naomi hope that Boaz would do as the family's kinsman-redeemer?

4 Look at Ruth 2:12 and 3:9 – how is Boaz going to be the answer to his own prayer?

5 Boaz knew he was the kinsman-redeemer, so why do you think he didn't act sooner?

HOW DOES THIS ... APPLY TO ME?

6 The custom of a kinsman-redeemer is an outdated one, but are there any principles we can learn from it about how to look after our families?

APPLY THIS TO ... MY CHURCH

7 How can these principles about looking after our natural families extend to caring for those in the church? Think specifically how your church can become more of an extended family instead of relative strangers who meet once a week.

8 Looking at your answers to question 2, how is Christ our kinsman-redeemer? Look up Psalm 121, Hebrews 13:5, Revelation 19:11.

WHAT DOES SEARCH THE BIBLE SAY? **9** God calls himself our redeemer. What does this mean for our lives? What has God done for us in this role of redeemer? Look at Exodus 6:6–8, Psalm 103:4, Isaiah 43:1, 44:22–23.

10 This chapter begins in v1 and ends in v18 speaking about 'rest' (the Hebrew word for 'home' in 3:1 is literally 'rest'). In what sense does finding our Redeemer give us true rest? Look at Psalm 62:1, Romans 5:1, Revelation 14:3.

11 Why do we as Christians often struggle with the concept of 'rest'? What can we do to combat this? Look at Ephesians 2:10.

WORSHIP

For the original readers of the Bible the word 'redeemer' would conjure up an image of slaves being 'redeemed' in the marketplace. A ransom was paid to set them free and rescue them from a life of slavery. As New Testament believers, the word creates another image in our minds – bread, wine and a cross. As you think again about the cost of your redemption, share communion together. Use your answers to questions 8 and 9 as starting points for your prayers of thanksgiving and praise.

FOR NEXT WEEK

God often asks us to be the answer to our own prayers, as Boaz was. Who or what situation are you praying for where you could be part of the answer? Ask God to help you as you give your prayers hands and feet this week.

DIFFICULT DECISIONS

Aim: To live by godly values so that we make wise decisions

Can you remember that decision which changed your life forever? Perhaps it was accepting a marriage proposal or rejecting one, applying for a job that changed the course of your career or going on a missions trip and seeing the world through new eyes. Often we forget that those big decisions are made up of many smaller choices, choices that are determined by our values and principles. So even if we can't predict the future, life's not all a game of chance – we can choose the values that shape our lives.

> *Meanwhile Boaz went up to the town gate and sat there. When the kinsman-redeemer he had mentioned came along, Boaz said, 'Come over here, my friend, and sit down.' So he went over and sat down.*
>
> *Boaz took ten of the elders of the town and said 'Sit here,' and they did so. Then he said to the kinsman-redeemer, 'Naomi, who has come back from Moab is selling the piece of land that belonged to our brother Elimelech. I thought I should bring the matter to your attention and suggest that you buy it in the presence of these seated here and in the presence of the elders of my people. If you will redeem it, do so. But if you will not, tell me, so I will know. For no one has the right to do it except you, and I am next in line.'*
>
> *'I will redeem it,' he said.*
>
> *Then Boaz said, 'On the day you buy the land from Naomi and from Ruth the Moabitess, you acquire the dead man's widow, in order to maintain the name of the dead with his property.'*
>
> *At this the kinsman-redeemer said, 'Then I cannot redeem it because I might endanger my own estate. You redeem it yourself. I cannot do it.'*
>
> ***Ruth 4:1–6***

TO SET THE SCENE

On an A4 sheet of paper take five minutes to list all the decisions you've made today from the time you got up until now. How many decisions did you make? Were they big or little decisions? To what extent was God central to your decision-making process?

READ RUTH 4:1-10

1 The author gives us the impression that Naomi is poverty-stricken, but in 4:3 we find out that she owns a field. Can you think of any explanation for this apparent mismatch?

2 Why did the closest kinsman-redeemer not want to buy the land?

3 What sacrifices was Boaz willing to make to marry Ruth?

4 The plot of the whole story and Ruth's future depends on this decision by the kinsman-redeemer.
- ▶ What values led Boaz to make the decision he did?
- ▶ What values led the other kinsman-redeemer to make the decision he did?

HOW DOES THIS / APPLY TO ME

5 Boaz didn't know the consequences of his decision – he didn't know that he would be the great-grandfather of King David! How does this encourage you in your decision-making?

6 Share together examples of when you have put your own needs aside for the sake of someone else. What was the outcome?

HOW DOES THIS / APPLY TO ME

7 What are the big decisions you're facing?

8 What priorities and values do you want to guide these decisions?

9 How do we put God at the centre of our decision-making process?

HOW DOES THIS **10** Often it's hard to know God's will when we're faced with two options that are both good. How do we know what God's best **APPLY TO ME** is? What steps have you found helpful to discern God's will? Look at Isaiah 30:21.

WORSHIP
Praise God for his sovereignty, that even though we may be anxious about the decisions we have to make and their consequences, God is in control. Read Job 38 together. Then, if you're facing a difficult decision (your answer from question 7) write it on a piece of paper and put it in a bowl. Set the papers alight to symbolise relinquishing your will in the situation and asking God to have his way. Pray in twos, asking God for wisdom to help you make these decisions.

FURTHER STUDY
There have been lots of books written about how to know God's will. One place to start is Sinclair B. Ferguson's short book called *Discovering God's Will*.

FOR NEXT WEEK
Continue to pray for the person you prayed with during the study. If it is appropriate, meet together during the week to pray or encourage each other by phone or email. Many of the situations you'll share in the group will be long term concerns, so be committed to each other!

ACTIVITY PAGE

We often have great difficulty in making decisions, and in finding and following God's will. Look at the following scenarios. Discuss the various factors that need to be taken into account and try and come up with a group decision on how you would advise these individuals.

> ▶ You're a youth leader and a girl in your youth group wants some career advice. She is bright and enjoys studying but is uncertain as to what career God wants her to embark on. She feels God may be calling her to be a missionary and has been offered a place at a university to read French and Spanish. She has also been offered a place to do Business Studies at a university nearer home and, as her parents aren't Christians, wonders whether she should stay close by so that she can maintain contact with them. What do you think?

> ▶ You have a very good job but the hours are long and demanding. You need to commute an hour each way to work and are away on numerous business trips spending a significant amount of time away from your young family. Various jobs have been advertised that are closer to home but none of them as secure as your present job. People in the church have questioned whether such time away from the family can be 'God's will'. Should you try and get a job closer to home or stay where you are?

> ▶ Your son is experimenting with steroids to improve his sporting skills. You have taken him to a counsellor and spoken to his coach but both seem to accept that this is normal behaviour. Your son is becoming less and less willing to listen to you. No other parents in church seem to be dealing with this type of issue and you feel isolated. How should you tackle your son's problem and your own feelings?

> ▶ Your eight-year-old daughter comes home from church and says that her friend's family has 'conferences' where they discuss everything from holidays to moving house to the parents having another baby. Your daughter asks what you think. What's your opinion? Should there be any boundaries to these conferences? As your daughter gets older, what should her role in family decision-making be? What will your role be in the decisions that she has to make?

FAMILY HERITAGE

AIM

Aim: To examine the spiritual heritage we've received and are passing on to the next generation

Every now and again we read in the newspapers about an old lady who's died and left her fortune to her cat! Perhaps you've been left something interesting in a relative's will – some jewellery, money or an embarrassing record collection. But we don't just leave material possessions when we die, do we? Whether we're rich or poor, we all leave a legacy – the influence we've had on people, the way our values and character have challenged them. What kind of legacy are you leaving?

> *So Boaz took Ruth and she became his wife. Then he went to her, and the Lord enabled her to conceive, and she gave birth to a son. The women said to Naomi: 'Praise be to the Lord, who this day has not left you without a kinsman-redeemer. May he become famous throughout Israel! He will renew your life and sustain you in your old age. For your daughter-in-law, who loves you and who is better to you than seven sons, has given him birth.'*
>
> *Then Naomi took the child, laid him in her lap and cared for him. The women living there said, 'Naomi has a son.' And they named him Obed. He was the father of Jesse, the father of David.*
>
> ***Ruth 4:13–17***

TO SET THE SCENE

Imagine you're being featured on the *This is Your Life* programme. The famous red book is about to be opened in front of all your family and friends. What three things do you hope will be emphasised? Choose one character trait, one personal/family achievement and one work/ministry achievement. Share your ideas with the group. You may also want to think about what information you hope won't be disclosed!

READ RUTH 4:11-22

1 Why were Rachel, Leah and Perez important figures in Israel's heritage?

2 How has Naomi's heritage changed throughout the course of the book?

3 Explain how Boaz and Ruth's family heritage had wider implications for the nation of Israel.

4 What blessings did the townsfolk pray for Ruth, Boaz and Obed?

5 Look at Paul's prayers to see what we can pray for others:
- ▶ Ephesians 1:15-23
- ▶ Ephesians 3:14-21
- ▶ Philippians 1:3-11
- ▶ Colossians 1:3-14

6 How do you feel about the fact that God's activity in your family may have wider implications?
- ▶ How does this help you view your struggles and suffering?
- ▶ How does this help you view the blessing and prosperity he's given you?

7 Many of us have had difficult family backgrounds that we wouldn't wish to pass on as a heritage to our children. Ruth and Boaz's decisions changed the course of their family history. How can we change the course of ours?

8 Think about your family heritage. What spiritual legacy do you want to pass on to your children? What practical measures can you put in place to make that happen?

9 Whether we have natural children or not, it is always possible to be a spiritual parent. Do you have someone you could mentor in the Christian faith? Someone you could pray a blessing on and encourage?

APPLY THIS TO
MY CHURCH

10 The church is a family. But it is only ever one generation away from extinction. What aspects do you need to work on so that your church has a spiritual legacy to pass on to the next generation? Think about:

▶ The age groups or sections of the church that need more input to grow spiritually
▶ The strategies for evangelism that need to be put in place
▶ The need for a greater emphasis on prayer
▶ The necessity of improving communication skills and techniques
▶ Aspects of leadership training that need to be put in place
▶ A greater emphasis given to teaching and discipleship
▶ Anything else?

Pray for your own particular church family.

WORSHIP
Thank God that our heritage and our future are in his hands. Praise him that we are now part of his family. You could meditate on these verses: John 1:12–13, Romans 8:16–17, 1 John 3:1–3. Then, in twos, pray a blessing on each other and on each other's families. Perhaps use Paul's prayers as a starting point.

FURTHER STUDY
There are many excellent books on prayer. For example *How to Pray for Lost Loved Ones* by Dutch Sheets gives some fresh ideas about praying for non-Christian family members.

FOR NEXT WEEK
Trace your own spiritual family tree. Who was your spiritual father or mother, who was most instrumental in leading you to Christ? Can you find out who their spiritual parent was? How far back in the family tree can you go? Thank God that he had his hand on your salvation since the beginning of time.

ACTIVITY PAGE

Christian families need a lot of prayer. Try setting up a special group, prayer triplets or incorporating more prayer for families in your regular church meetings.

Pray through issues that are relevant to your own particular church and community situation. Here are some topics to help you get started:

- Wisdom to know how to live and share the gospel with unbelieving family members
- Single parent families in the church
- Parenting Classes, Tots and Toys groups etc run by your church
- The families of those heavily involved in church leadership
- Wisdom for the various stages of parenting
- Christian young people facing peer pressure at school and university

If you need more resources you could contact Care for the Family.

A HAPPY ENDING

Aim: To reflect on the lessons in the book of Ruth

There isn't much good news these days. Tales of loyalty and courage are reserved for special award shows or fantasy films. But the story of Ruth breaks the trend – it demonstrates love and devotion being rewarded in tangible ways and emphasises the value of living by God's standards. As we reflect on the lessons in this book we're reminded that above all else we trust in a God who acts in the everyday affairs of men and women.

> *Then Naomi took the child, laid him in her lap and cared for him. The women living there said, 'Naomi has a son.' And they named him Obed. He was the father of Jesse, the father of David.*
>
> *This, then, is the family line of Perez:*
>
> *Perez was the father of Hezron,*
> *Hezron the father of Ram,*
> *Ram the father of Amminadab,*
> *Amminadab the father of Nahshon,*
> *Nahshon the father of Salmon,*
> *Salmon the father of Boaz*
> *Boaz the father of Obed,*
> *Obed the father of Jesse,*
> *And Jesse the father of David.*

Ruth 4:16–22

TO SET THE SCENE
When is the last time you heard a story like Ruth's, one with a happy ending? Share together true stories or examples from books and films where something good comes out of a bad situation. Can you come up with a top five list of films or books with a happy ending?

READ THROUGH THE BOOK OF RUTH

1   As you read through the book again, try to come up with a headline for each chapter. Think of something that would grab people's attention and encourage them to read on.

2   What are the key themes in the story?

3   The book gives us many images of God but which one means the most to you? Think about:
- God our refuge
- God our husband
- God our redeemer
- God our provider
- God our inheritance

4   In the context of the Old Testament, what contribution does this small book make?

5   Divide into four groups and have each group look at one chapter of the book. Make a list of all God's actions in the story, even if they are attributed to another character or to fate.

6   What principles can you learn from this story about how God works?

 7   What difference do these principles make to your life?

 8   Can you see these principles in operation in your church and community?

 9   How do the lessons of this book make you want to change? Think about:
- Your actions/attitude towards God
- Your actions/attitude toward others

WORSHIP

Spend time praising God for all that we learn about him in the book of Ruth (use your thoughts on question 3 as a starting point). Praise him for his unseen hand, not only at work in Ruth's life but also in ours. We may not always have the happy ending we wanted and life may turn out very differently to what we'd intended, but we know that in ways we can't always discern God is acting for our good and his glory. Imagine your life not pulled by puppet strings but resting in the hollow of God's hand. Meditate on these verses: Psalm 37:23–24, 139:9–10, Isaiah 40:12, 48:13, and 49:16 where we learn more about the Master's hands.

FOR FUTURE WEEKS

Tell a friend or prayer partner your answer to question 9. Explain to them the lessons you've learnt from the book of Ruth and the ways God's challenging you to grow as a result. Invite them to ask you at regular intervals how much progress you're making towards these goals and be honest!

ACTIVITY PAGE

'For my thoughts are not your thoughts, neither are your ways my ways,' declares the Lord.

The way God thinks and acts in human history has caused much controversy among Christians and non-Christians. Think through how you would respond to the following scenarios.

▶ A non-Christian tells you that the God of the Bible is not consistent because on some occasions he intervenes dramatically, at other times he uses human means and at others he declines to intervene at all. The person concludes that as God's character is so pragmatic he can't be trusted. Therefore the whole basis for Christianity and accepting the Bible as authentic is flawed. He cites the contrast between a God who dramatically opens the Red Sea for the Israelites but at the same time wouldn't stop David and Bathsheba's baby son from dying.

▶ Your friend has been a Christian for eighteen months. When they were first converted, God answered their prayers very dramatically. God even seemed to answer prayers that you felt were rather trivial. For example, once they prayed that God would send them a friend to meet them at the door of the church so they wouldn't need to go in alone – and God answered their request. But recently your friend has become despondent because God doesn't seem to be answering their prayers in the same way. Your friend feels God has left them or at least gone silent. What would you say?

▶ A friend in your housegroup rings you up. These studies have made her anxious. In the book of Ruth God has worked through everyday routine events, chance occurrences and the decisions of others to further his purpose. Your friend is worried that if God uses such everyday means to accomplish his important plans, how will she be able to discern his hand? If the washing machine breaks down or she has an interesting conversation with another mother at the school gate, how can she discern whether God means something consequential to come out of it or whether it's just meant to be part of the fabric of life? How can she relax and get on making everyday decisions, knowing that God could have some big plan behind every one of her rushed choices?

LEADERS' GUIDE

TO HELP YOU LEAD

You may have led a housegroup many times before or this may be your first time. Here is some advice on how to lead these studies:

▶ As a group leader, you don't have to be an expert or a lecturer. You are there to facilitate the learning of the group members – helping them to discover for themselves the wisdom in God's word. You should not be doing most of the talking or dishing out the answers, whatever the group expects from you!

▶ You do need to be aware of the group's dynamics, however. People can be quite quick to label themselves and each other in a group situation. One person might be seen as the expert, another the moaner who always has something to complain about. One person may be labelled as quiet and not be expected to contribute; another person may always jump in with something to say. Be aware of the different type of individuals in the group, but don't allow the labels to stick. You may need to encourage those who find it hard to get a word in, and quieten down those who always have something to say. Talk to members between sessions to find out how they feel about the group.

▶ The sessions are planned to try and engage every member in active learning. Of course you cannot force anyone to take part if they don't want to, but it won't be too easy to be a spectator. Activities that ask everyone to write down a word, or talk in twos, and then report back to the group are there for a reason. They give everyone space to think and form their opinion, even if not everyone voices it out loud.

▶ Do adapt the sessions for your group as you feel is appropriate. Some groups may know each other very well and will be prepared to talk at a deep level. New groups may take a bit of time to get to know each other before making themselves vulnerable, but encourage members to share their lives with each other.

▶ You probably won't be able to tackle all the questions in each session so decide in advance which ones are most appropriate to your group and situation.

▶ Encourage a number of replies to each question. The study is not about finding a single right answer, but about sharing experiences and thoughts in order to find out how to apply the Bible to people's lives. When brainstorming, don't be too quick to evaluate the contributions. Write everything down and then have a look to see which suggestions are worth keeping.

▶ Similarly encourage everyone to ask questions, voice doubts and discuss difficulties. Some parts of the Bible are difficult to understand. Sometimes the Christian faith throws up paradoxes. Painful things happen to us that make it difficult to see what God is doing. A housegroup should be a safe place to express all of this. If discussion doesn't resolve the issue, send everyone away to pray about it between sessions, and ask your minister for advice.

▶ Give yourself time in the week to read through the Bible passage and the questions. Read the Leaders' notes for the session, as different ways of presenting the questions are sometimes suggested. However, during the session don't be too quick to come in with the answer – sometimes people need space to think.

▶ Delegate as much as you like! The easiest activities to delegate are reading the text, and the worship sessions, but there are other ways to involve the group members. Giving people responsibility can help them own the session much more.

▶ Pray for group members by name, that God would meet with them during the week. Pray for the group session, for a constructive and helpful time. Ask the Lord to equip you as you lead the group.

THE STRUCTURE OF EACH SESSION

Feedback: find out what people remember from the previous session, or if they have been able to act during the week on what was discussed last time.

To set the scene: an activity or a question to get everyone thinking about the subject to be studied.

Bible reading: it's important actually to read the passage you are studying during the session. Ask someone to prepare this in advance or go around the group reading a verse or two each. Don't assume everyone will be happy to read out loud.

Questions and activities: adapt these as appropriate to your group. Some groups may enjoy a more activity-based approach; some may prefer just to discuss the questions. Try out some new things!

Worship: suggestions for creative worship and prayer are included, which give everyone an opportunity to respond to God, largely individually. Use these alongside singing or other group expressions of worship. Add a prayer time with opportunities to pray for group members and their families and friends.

For next week: this gives a specific task to do during the week, helping people to continue to think about or apply what they have learned.

Further study: suggestions are given for those people who want to study the themes further. These could be included in the housegroup if you feel it's appropriate and if there is time.

WHAT YOU NEED

A list of materials that are needed is printed at the start of each session in the Leaders' Guide. In addition you will probably need:

Bibles: the main Bible passage is printed in the book so that all the members can work from the same version. It is useful to have other Bibles available, or to ask everyone to bring their own, so that other passages can be referred to.

Paper and Pens: for people who need more space than is in the book!

Flip chart: it is helpful to write down people's comments during a brainstorming session, so that none of the suggestions are lost. There may not be space for a proper flip chart in the average lounge, and having one may make it feel too much like a business meeting or lecture. Try getting someone to write on a big sheet of paper on the floor or coffee table, and then stick this up on the wall with blu-tack.

GROUND RULES

How do people know what is expected of them in a housegroup situation? Is it ever discussed, or do we just pick up clues from each other? You may find it helpful to discuss some ground rules for the housegroup at the start of this course, even if your group has been going a long time. This also gives you an opportunity to talk about how you, as the leader, see the group. Ask everyone to think about what they want to get out of the course. How do they want the group to work? What values do they want to be part of the group's experience; honesty, respect, confidentiality? How do they want their contributions to be treated? You could ask everyone to write down three ground rules on slips of paper and put them in a bowl. Pass the bowl around the group. Each person takes out a rule and reads it, and someone collates the list. Discuss the ground rules that have been suggested and come up with a top five. This method enables everyone to contribute fairly anonymously. Alternatively, if your group are all quite vocal, have a straight discussion about it!

NB — Not all questions in each session are covered, some are self-explanatory.

ICONS

The aim of the session

Engaging with the world

Investigate what else the Bible says

How does this apply to me?

What about my church?

www.springharvest.org/workbooks/

SESSION 1

TO SET THE SCENE

If this is the first time you've met as a group, introduce yourselves. With this opening exercise of the series, allow people to be as open as they feel comfortable being. They don't need to refer to a crisis on the scale of Naomi's, just any difficulty they have struggled with. Invite people to explain simply how they coped with their difficulty or describe the whole situation – whatever suits them. Finding out what helps individuals cope well in hard times will help you care for each other more effectively in the future.

If you have time, read through the book of Ruth together – perhaps with individuals reading the part of a character. If this is not possible, encourage your group members to read the book on their own during the week.

1   The Israelites hadn't removed the Canaanites from the Promised Land as God had told them, so they faced oppression from their enemies. They copied their religious practices and followed their gods, declining morally and spiritually. The frequent refrain throughout the book of Judges is 'In those days Israel had no king; everyone did as he saw fit.' They had abandoned God as their king so he allowed them to be taken over by their enemies. When the people repented God sent a judge to deliver them – Gideon or Samson, for example. But even the judges weren't paragons of virtue! (For more details read the Introduction to this study guide.)

2   'Empty' is a good description of Naomi. She had left Bethlehem because her stomach was empty, but though she found food in Moab she was now emotionally empty because her husband and sons had died. She had to face not only the grief but also the practical reality of being 'empty' – men were the money earners in the family so she was destitute and she now had no male to protect and care for her.

3   God obviously permitted Naomi's relatives to die but he did not cause it. He did not strike them down. Rather, death came as a result of natural causes i.e. the common results of sin in the world. Nevertheless, it is hard for Naomi to accept that the sovereign, all-powerful God would choose not to intervene. It is only later that she recognises that God did act on her behalf. At this point in the story, however, Naomi's reaction is understandable as she is coming to terms with her grief and anticipating a dismal future.

4 God may bring difficulties into our lives to discipline and correct us. He may use them to test our faith as he did with Job. Difficulties may simply be the result of our sinfulness or the consequences of living in a fallen world. We need to examine our hearts and ask God if we need to repent, learn a lesson or simply trust him through the experience.

5 Naomi felt that Ruth could have started a new life in Moab. She could have remarried, had children and stayed near her own relatives for support. By coming to Bethlehem, there were now two destitute widows needing support and no obvious means to obtain it. Although there was a temporary peace between Moab and Israel (Judg. 3:12–30) there was the possibility that Ruth wouldn't have been warmly welcomed in Bethlehem.

6 Encourage people to be as honest as possible. Split up into groups of twos or threes if this would make conversation easier.

7 Ruth's loyalty to her mother-in-law (v16–17) and her commitment to God are a sign of hope, given the backdrop of the period of the judges. Naomi mentions God's sovereignty in verses 20–21, reminding the reader that however she felt and however bleak the situation seemed to be, God was still in control. Verse 22: the women return to Bethlehem just as the barley harvest was starting – a hint that they would not be 'empty' for long.

8 Encourage people to apply these verses to the specifics of their own situations.

9 The church's response largely depends on the nature of the crisis, so try and get the group to reflect on issues pertinent to your church. This could mean running a parenting course for parents of teenagers, speaking publicly about substance abuse, having a meal and practical help rota for those with financial hardships, providing debt counselling, having prayer groups set up specifically to pray for church families.

WORSHIP

Be sensitive: some may be going through crises where they find it very difficult to see God's love and goodness. Others may not want to share their hurts, and for others life may be going fine! Decide how to handle this section of the study depending on the nature of the group and how well you know each other.

SESSION 2

MATERIALS NEEDED

Flip chart or large piece of paper and pens for the brainstorming session in the Setting the Scene exercise

A4 sheets of paper and pens for Question 9

CDs, tapes, music system or instruments available for the worship session if necessary

TO SET THE SCENE

You may come up with a general definition but encourage people to recognise that kindness means different things in different situations and to different people. As for the people who show us kindness – it often depends on the issue, who is geographically closer, whether they can identify with our need, whether we share our need with them etc. Move the discussion on to whom the individual group members show kindness to most readily – are people insensitive to the needs of others? Why? How can we change?

1   Ruth returned to Bethlehem to look after Naomi rather than staying in her homeland of Moab. Boaz invited Ruth to keep collecting grain in his field, to work alongside his servant girls; he gave her protection, offered her water to drink and a meal, and instructed his men to pull out extra heads of barley from the sheaves so she had more grain to take home. These were special privileges: for instance, water was so valuable it wouldn't normally be offered to gleaners. In 2:8, he says the same thing three times – essentially 'Stay in my field.'

2   Ruth was giving up her security by going to Bethlehem. It would have been much easier for her to stay in Moab where she could have married, had children and the support of her own family. Instead two widows in Bethlehem had no potential for earning money, no protection and security, and by allying herself with Naomi, Ruth was unlikely to find a husband who would look after both of them. At least this is the scenario from a human point of view!

3 God works behind the scenes to bring about his purposes. He uses the decisions taken by the characters – such as Ruth deciding to go gleaning and Naomi assenting to this, and Boaz's kindnesses towards Ruth. He is also behind the apparent coincidences – Ruth just happened to be working in Boaz's field, he decides to harvest the field that day, he notices Ruth and turns out to be a relative of the family with special responsibilities for them.

4 The nation of Moab had its origin in a drunken one-night stand between Lot and his older daughter. Probably because of these immoral origins and because the Moabites were fierce enemies of Israel, they were not allowed into the assembly of the Lord. 'Down to the tenth generation' probably is a way of saying 'forever'.

5 Ruth became part of the family of God because she committed herself to the God of Israel. She turned her back on the ways of her ancestors and was willing to be obedient to God's will, submitting herself to his sovereignty. This is clearly demonstrated by her loyalty to Naomi.

6 Protection, care, security, refuge, God's power extends to cover us. The term speaks of the refuge God offers us in salvation but also the protection and care he provides on an ongoing basis. He wants to look after us like a hen cares for her chicks (Lk. 13:34).

7 God is the God of Israel but he gave refuge to a Moabitess. This is a reminder that all can find refuge in God, regardless of religious background or experience if they repent and trust in him. Christianity is not an exclusive club open to just us and our friends – it is a club which exists for the benefit of its non-members! As individuals and as a church, we need to be sharing the gospel with all who will listen, looking for new ways into our communities and reaching people and social groups that others have rejected.

8 We shouldn't just be kind to people so that we will earn the right to share the gospel with them. But at the same time we shouldn't underestimate the effect of our kindness to each other and to outsiders (Jn. 13:35). Kindness helps build relationships with non-Christians, it shows a care that people do not often experience outside their families, and it shows the genuineness of our faith. For example, providing a free meal at *Discovering Christianity* or *Alpha* courses often encourages people to ask why Christians go to so much effort to share their faith.

SESSION 3

MATERIALS NEEDED:
Bread and wine if you are sharing communion together

Flip chart or large sheets of paper and pens for the brainstorming in question 1

TO SET THE SCENE
This exercise is intended to introduce one of the themes of the redeemer/kinsman-redeemer concept. Perhaps by sharing 'rescue accounts' you'll learn things about the group that you wouldn't otherwise have know.

1   To 'redeem' literally means to buy back from slavery. It has the connotations of rescue and ransom. You could explain the slave market practice where someone paid to secure a slave's freedom. Jesus' death paid the penalty for our sin, so we are now free to enjoy a relationship with God and free to go to heaven. You could use images such as redeeming something from a pawnshop or posting a bond to secure someone's bail, paying the ransom to rescue someone – although these illustrations cannot be pressed too far.

2   The kinsman-redeemer was responsible for needy relatives – for buying back land they'd sold outside the family in times of financial hardship, for buying them out of slavery, for avenging their murder, and for providing an heir for a brother who had died.

3   Naomi was hoping that Boaz would marry Ruth and not only look after her and Ruth but also provide an heir who would continue her dead son's line (Deut. 25:5–6).

4   Boaz asks God, in whom Ruth had found refuge, to reward her for her kindness to Naomi. He becomes the answer to his own prayer when Ruth asks Boaz to cover her with his garment. She is asking him to let her find refuge in him, i.e. to marry her. The wings of the Lord and the wings of Boaz's garments are the same word in Hebrew.

5   Boaz was slow to act because he knew there was a kinsman-redeemer who was a closer relative (3:12) and because he thought that Ruth would prefer a younger husband (3:10). Your group may come up with other ideas.

6 There are obviously some principles we wouldn't advocate copying, such as avenging the killing of a relative! However, the concept of a kinsman-redeemer underlines the importance of family loyalty, protecting and supporting individuals within the family. Often there is the tendency to leave financial support, education and care to other agencies and perhaps the kinsman-redeemer concept should challenge us as to the role of families and the church family in this regard.

7 The church should be a place where there is loyalty and support for individuals, where those in need find help and protection. Like Boaz, we should welcome the lonely, the foreigners, those who have found life difficult. We should be God's hands and feet to these people, proving to them that God's justice and kindness are a reality. Church can also become more of an extended family as we develop relationships by working together on specific projects, meeting together in small groups, praying for each other's needs, and finding ways to share our lives.

8 Christ's death on the cross has bought us back from slavery; he rescues us from the penalty and power of sin; he protects us (Ps. 121); he promises always to be faithful to us (Heb. 13:5); he gives us a heritage (eternal life and heaven to look forward to); he promises to avenge those who hurt us and to bring justice on the final judgement day (Rev. 19:11).

9 God showed himself as a redeemer when he rescued the Israelites from slavery in Egypt – he did on a national scale what the kinsman-redeemer did for an individual (Ex. 6:6–8). This redemption of the Israelites was a picture of the redemption that God, through Christ, offers to those who put their trust in him. He gives us eternal life so that we don't ever die spiritually (Ps. 103:4). Subsequently we too now belong to God and he knows us intimately (Is. 43:1). Our sins are forgiven and we can experience a sense of joy because God is glorified by the personal transformation his redemption brings to our lives (Is. 44:22–23).

10 When we become Christians we find rest for our souls because we're no longer searching for a meaning and significance to life – we've discovered the reason we were made (Ps. 62:1). We find rest in the sense that we receive eternal life now, our relationship with God is restored, and we have peace (Rom. 5:1). We also look forward to eternal rest in heaven when we'll be free from the struggles of sin and the problems of living in a fallen world (Rev. 14:13).

11 We find 'rest' difficult because we want to be doing the works God has planned for us (Eph. 2:10) but too often we get caught up in the busyness of service rather than living for God. We tend to see our significance in what we are doing for God rather than what he has done for us. We can lose the feeling, although not the reality, of peace with God if we don't spend time in his presence. To appreciate the rest we have in God we need to give ourselves time alone with him to meditate and pray, we need to find ways to keep our focus on him rather than on our service. Discuss how this could work in practice.

WORSHIP
In some cases, it might be appropriate to mention to your minister about your wish to share communion together as a group. Adapt this section to your church setting.

SESSION 4

MATERIALS NEEDED:
A4 sheets of paper and pens for the Setting the Scene exercise

Paper, pens, a bowl and matches if you are going to follow the suggestions for the worship session

TO SET THE SCENE
We don't realise how many choices and decisions we make in a day. We usually consult God on the big decisions but what about the little ones? Use this opportunity to discuss how we can incorporate God and a God-shaped worldview in the regular, everyday decisions we make.

1 It is possible that Naomi owned a field but couldn't harvest it herself as she was a woman; and couldn't sell it until now because caretakers were harvesting their own crops on it – either way she could still be destitute. Possibly Elimelech had sold the field before he went to Moab but the family still held the right of redemption. In both scenarios, Naomi needed a kinsman-redeemer so that the land did not pass outside the family.

2 Initially the kinsman-redeemer did want to buy the land because it would increase his wealth. But the financial drain of providing for Ruth, any children she might have, and her mother-in-law far outweighed the value of the land. Also if a child of Ruth's was the only heir this kinsman-redeemer had, all his property would transfer to the family of Elimelech and his own line would die out.

3 Boaz was willing to make all the sacrifices that the other kinsman-redeemer wouldn't – he paid for the land; was willing to look after Ruth, any children she might have, and Naomi; and to allow his heir to be legally thought of as Mahlon's.

4 Boaz was motivated by care for Ruth and Naomi, admiration for Ruth's sacrifice (2:11), a sense of God's justice and protection (2:12), a sense of his own family responsibility as kinsman-redeemer (3:13, 4:9–10), as well as being impressed by Ruth's loyalty to him and her noble character (3:10,11). The kinsman-redeemer decided not to buy the field because he was motivated by personal financial concerns and a wish to preserve his own family line (4:6). Boaz seems to be motivated by moral values, his decision was based on his, Ruth's and God's character, whereas the other kinsman-redeemer responded pragmatically and practically to the situation.

5 The story of Ruth encourages us that even though we often can't see the outcome of our decisions, we can still make wise choices if we are living by godly values and acting from a godly character.

6 Individuals may give examples of times where God has rewarded their integrity and also times where making godly choices does not appear to have paid off – encourage each other that these choices are still wise and God is still working behind the scenes!

7 Discuss this question in twos if you feel it would be more appropriate.

8 Encourage people to see that we don't just make decisions *ad hoc* but we do so from a framework, a worldview. The challenge as Christians is to cultivate a God-centred worldview where values like integrity, honesty, the good of others, justice, loyalty, being like Jesus etc become inherent in us and so, even subconsciously, guide not only the big decisions but also the routine ones.

9 We put God at the centre of our decision-making process by cultivating a God-centred worldview. This means spending time with God, his word, and his people. By looking at Jesus' character and how God treats and reacts to people and situations, we can start to share his values and shape our life by godly principles.

10 We can discern God's will from his word, from advice from godly leaders, a sense of peace in our spirits, and whether doors of opportunity open or shut for us. When two decisions seem equally good, perhaps, we need to work through the logic of the decisions. If, after much prayer, they both seem right then we should just make a choice and ask God to close the door for us if he doesn't want us to proceed (Is. 30:21). At times it is perhaps not so much the decision we make as our heart behind it which matters most to God.

SESSION 5

TO SET THE SCENE

This exercise is designed to help the group members think about the type of heritage they do and don't want to pass on to the next generation. We may have dreams of what might be revealed on *This is Your Life* but we need to face up to reality and think how we can make our legacy more positive. Encourage the group to be honest with their three revelations. Remember that the 'achievements' part doesn't need to be achievements everyone would recognise as significant, only things that are significant to you.

1 Rachel and Leah were the mothers of the twelve men who became the leaders of the tribes of Israel. These matriarchs are mentioned in the genealogy because they were formative in Israel's history, their fruitfulness built a strong nation. Perez was the child of a union between Judah and Tamar that was similar to the arrangement between Ruth and Boaz. Perez was an ancestor of Boaz and his descendants became the tribe of Judah. Perez is mentioned by the elders because they wanted Boaz to have an equally influential family line.

2 Naomi described herself as 'empty' (1:21) – she had no family and was destitute. She had no heritage but, by the end of the story, her situation has changed completely. She is part of a loving family, is nursing her grandchild and described as having a 'son' (4:14–17). One would have thought that seven sons would have provided Naomi with a blessed heritage but it turned out that having Ruth as a daughter-in-law was better than that! Naomi's family heritage was carried on through the line of Christ.

3 Ruth and Boaz's child was precious to them but was also part of God's bigger plan of salvation. Obed became an ancestor of King David, from whom Christ was descended. This genealogy indicates that Christ was part of God's plan from before the beginning of time. The Israelites reading the book of Ruth would recall that just as Naomi had found rest, they too had found peace and rest under King David in the Promised Land.

4 For Ruth they prayed for fruitfulness; for Boaz they prayed for integrity and good character; for Obed they prayed for fame, that he would be well-known and held in high regard.

5 In Ephesians 1:15–23, Paul prayed for wisdom and revelation so that we might know God better, that we might realise the full extent of our inheritance and the spiritual power we have access to. In Ephesians 3:14–21, he prayed for God's power so that Christ would be fully at home in our lives, that we would know God's love and be filled to overflowing with God. In Philippians 1:3–11, his prayer was one of thankfulness for the believers' faithfulness in the gospel; he prayed their love would become mature and insightful so that they could discern God's best and live blameless lives. In Colossians 1:3–14, he thanked God for their faith, love and hope and prayed that God would help them live fruitful lives that pleased him and they would endure hardship and be thankful. Notice that generally Paul prayed for their spiritual development rather than the material, health or career concerns that we often major on.

6 People may come up with a variety of answers here. Perhaps knowing that there is a bigger picture helps us cope with suffering, because we know it is part of God's plan (i.e. Jesus had a reason for not rushing to heal Lazarus: John 11:4, 14). Knowing that our blessings and prosperity are part of a bigger plan also brings a responsibility. We need to ensure that we use wisely and share all that has been given to us.

7 Knowing the mistakes of the past that we don't want to repeat is important but we can also try to change our family heritage through prayer, following godly role models, and gaining the support of others. We can break the cycle of what is communicated to the next generation if we look after our own relationship with God and seek to love and serve him fully (Rom. 12:2).

8 Try and get the group to be specific about the spiritual heritage they want to pass on and to come up with practical measures to put in place – for example, having a family devotional time, saying prayers with your children, talking with them about spiritual things rather than just leaving it to Sunday School teachers.

LEADERS' GUIDE

SESSION 6

MATERIALS NEEDED:
A flip chart or large sheets of paper and pens may be helpful as you discuss some of the questions in this session.

TO SET THE SCENE
This fun exercise will help you get to know each other better as you hear about people's taste in books and films.

1 Titles could be –
Chapter 1: 'Triple tragedy strikes immigrant family'
Chapter 2: 'Local man saves the day for two desolate widows'
Chapter 3: 'Romance blossoms in the most unlikely places'
Chapter 4: 'The field that held hidden treasures'

2 There are numerous themes to the story. For example – God's hand working behind the scenes, prayer and blessings, God's protection and redemption, loyalty and loving-kindness, family, tragedy, decisions, kinsman-redeemer, and a foreigner becoming part of the family of God.

3 Ask group members to explain why a particular image is precious to them.

4 The book of Ruth demonstrates that in a context of moral and spiritual decay, there were still righteous individuals that God used to further his plan of redemption. The book is a reminder of God's work behind the scenes of our lives and that he rewards integrity and covenant loyalty.

5 Examples of God at work:
Chapter 1 – there was a harvest in Bethlehem and Ruth decided to return with Naomi.
Chapter 2 – Boaz happened to be a kinsman of Elimelech, Ruth decided to go and collect grain, Naomi let her, Ruth just happened to go to work in Boaz's field, Boaz happened to be harvesting the field that day, he spotted her and was very gracious to her.
Chapter 3 – Naomi encouraged Ruth to present herself to Boaz, Ruth agreed, and Boaz consented to act as a kinsman-redeemer.

Chapter 4 – the other kinsman-redeemer declined to buy the field, leaving Boaz to do so and to marry Ruth. She conceived Obed, who was an ancestor in the line of Christ.

6 We learn that God works in the ordinary events and daily decisions of life. In the book of Ruth, God didn't intervene dramatically in a miraculous way but accomplished his plan through human decisions and actions. He used the loyalty and faithfulness of his servants to achieve his will.

7 We can be encouraged that even if God doesn't intervene dramatically he is still in control, still at work in our lives – even if it doesn't seem like it and our lives don't have the happy ending that Ruth's did. We have a responsibility to maintain and develop our relationship with the Lord so that we live righteously and so that he can work through the decisions that we make. God didn't reveal his bigger plan to the characters and this reminds us to be faithful because we don't know how God will use our lives for his glory.

8 Your group may be able to come up with examples of how God has worked in the background to achieve his purpose in the church or community. Perhaps you can only see with hindsight how God has used individuals and circumstances to further his plans. For example, it would have been much more dramatic and easier if God had encouraged the council to give you permission to build a new church building ten years ago but now with hindsight you see how those years were important to build up the individuals in the church, to develop a relationship with the council and to build bridges into the community.

WORSHIP
As this is the last in this series of studies, make sure you leave enough time for people to make their personal responses, to reflect on what they have learnt about God and what he has challenged them about.

FURTHER READING AND INFORMATION

The book of Ruth brings up many issues that you might like to look at further. Here is a list of books to help you get started:

The Problem of Pain – C. S. Lewis
Disappointment with God – Philip Yancey
The Five Love Languages – Gary Chapman
Sixty Minute Father – Rob Parsons
Sixty Minute Mother – Rob Parsons
How to Pray for Lost Loved Ones – Dutch Sheets
Prayer – O. Hallesby
Listening to God – Joyce Huggett
Discovering God's Will – Sinclair B. Ferguson

If you would like further information and resources, the following organisations may be of help. They will be able to tell you what is going on in your locality and how you can get involved:

The Evangelical Alliance
186 Kennington Park Road,
London SE11 4BT
Tel: 020 7207 2100 Email: info@eauk.org.

Care for the Family
PO Box 488
Cardiff CF15 7YY
Tel: 02920 810800 Email: mail@cff.org.uk

Faithworks
Tel: 0207 450 9050
www.faithworkscampaign.org

Open Doors
PO Box 6
Witney
Oxon OX29 6WG
Tel: 01993 885400 Email: helpdesk@opendoorsuk.org

Rebuild
16 Kingston Road
London SW19 1JZ
Tel: 020 82395581 Email: info@rebuild.org.uk

TEARFUND
100 Church Road
Teddington TW11 8QE
Tel: 020 8977 9144   www.tearfund.org

London Institute for Contemporary Christianity
Tel: 0207 3999555   www.licc.org.uk

www.springharvest.org/workbooks/